MY LITTLE GYMNAST

Series 1

Mar and Jaq

Start Gymnastics School

Marty Urand

Copyright © Case # 1-12465200681

All rights reserved. No part of this publication may be produced, distributed, or transmitted in any form or by any means, including photocopying, recording, or other electronic or mechanical methods, without the prior written permission of the published, except in the case of brief quotations embodied in critical reviews and other noncommercial uses permitted by copyright law.

ISBN: (Paperback) 978-1-916954-44-1
ISBN: (Hardcover) 978-1-916954-45-8

The views expressed in this book are solely those of the author and do not necessarily reflect the views of the publisher, and the publisher hereby disclaims any responsibility for them.

USA

Urand Sports Association, Inc.

Urand@ymail.com

Dedication

A big thanks to Pamela Urand for her time and insight for this publication ~ thank you!

Acknowledgment

Life was wonderful with much joy that my family extended to me. To my wife of fifty-two years (Passed 2018) Deanna, and my wonderful daughters, Marti and Jacqui.

My daughters, for the most part, grew up in a gym while Deanna was close by running the business at the front desk. Each day we arrived at the Gymnastic club by 3:30 and the girls accomplished their daily homework while waiting for their team work out that began at 6:00 and lasted to 9:00 PM. Dinner was mostly fast-food caliber with a snack when we arrived home.

By the time we arrived home, it was pushing 9:30 PM. Bedtime came quick and we were out the door by 7:00 AM. It was a brutal schedule for our family and especially for our daughters. It must have not been that life threatening as both girls attended college. Marti, graduated from Texas A&M and Jacqui, from Sam Houston University.

This routine lasted from their second/third grade through first year of high school. Needless to say, I have always been very proud of my family for buying into my career as a coach/gym owner that lasted until each married and began a life that in my eyes, was certainly less stressful as well as healthy~

Table of Contents

Dedication i

Acknowledgment ii

About the Author iv

Chapter 1: Learning Gymnastics at Ashford Elementary School 1

Chapter 2: Russian Tour Workout 7

Chapter 3: Joining a Gymnastic Club 10

Chapter 4: Ashford Elementary School Focuses on A New Event . 14

Chapter 5: Overnight Campout Big Success 18

Chapter 6: Shamrock Demonstration 19

Chapter 7: Extraordinary Tumbling Routine "Live and Let Die" ... 22

Chapter 8: First Day of Gymnastic School 24

Chapter 9: A New Elementary School 27

Chapter 10: Mar & Jaq Change Gymnastic Clubs 28

Chapter 11: A New Gymnastic Club for Katy, Texas 29

Chapter 12: West Memorial Elementary School Receives an Outstanding Award 32

Series 2: Mar & Jaq Compete in their First Meet 33

About the Author

Martin "Marty" Urand is a graduate of the University of Texas Rio Grande Valley in Edinburg, Texas. After an initial coaching career in high school and college basketball, he received his Master's degree in Kinesiology from Sam Houston University in Huntsville, Texas. Marty began his esteemed teaching career as a high school and college basketball coach. Providence intervenes, giving Marty opportunities to follow his life's work to teach Physical Education at the elementary school level.

As a dedicated teacher in his first pivotal elementary school coaching position, Marty wanted to provide all students with an after-school recreation program. However, all the boys were involved with football and baseball. This situation offered the girls a place in the gym to come and practice recreational games. The girls wanted more than trivial games and requested to learn gymnastics. Without a background in that sport, Marty judiciously required that his student teachers have a gymnastic background (so he could learn gymnastics from them.) He befriended Coach Beau Biron from Biron's "Bee Gees" Gymnastic Club in Houston, Texas, and in short order began teaching gymnastics at Biron's club. "Beau was instrumental in my education of this new sport, and I am very appreciative."

Marti is his first daughter, and Jacqui is the second. They both inherited athletic skills and had an exceptional gymnastics career.

Marti graduated from Texas A&M University, and Jacqui from Sam Houston State University. Both daughters currently reside in the Houston area, are married, have families of their own, and are successful businesswomen.

Marty "Coach U" resides in the Conroe area with his wife Pamela and is a doting grandfather, 2013 Professor of the Year recipient, and adjunct professor at Lone Star College.

Chapter 1:
Learning Gymnastics at Ashford Elementary School

Coach U, the father of Mar & Jaq, was the PE Teacher at Ashford Elementary School when the girls began school. When Coach U began his after-school recreation program, he noticed the boys outside practicing football and baseball. Most of the students in the gym were girls and were becoming bored with jump rope, hula hoops, hopscotch, and various floor games such as Four Square.

One afternoon, Coach U asked all the girls and the few boys in the gym, "Okay, students, I know you say you are bored with these non-competitive activities. What game or sport do you want to learn?" And they all replied, "Gymnastics."

OK! Here it is…this magical moment, the critical juncture- the climactic, defining moment when gymnastics became "a gleam in Coach U's eyes."

However, along with the inspiration comes the challenges. Ashford was a new school and did not have any tumbling mats or any safe equipment that could be used for gymnastics.

The next day, during Coach U's gym classes, he makes an imploring plea to his students, "Listen up, everyone. Here's your first and probably only homework this year. When you get home after school today, be sure to ask your parents or guardians if they have or know anyone with tumbling mats they would be willing to let the school use until we purchase our own."

Meanwhile, located only two miles away from the school is Biron Gymnastics. Coach U goes to Biron's and asks the owner, Beau Biron if he has a few old mats that he could loan the school until they purchase some mats.

On the spot, Coach Biron donates six mats and a vaulting box to the school! The students write Coach Biron and thank him for his generosity and support of their new program. Coach U also secures a date and time on the schedule for Biron's tumbling team to visit and perform a gymnastics demonstration for the Ashford students!

Within a month's time, several students become so good at gymnastics that these students are selected by the after-school group to become the "Gymnastic Leaders" to help Coach U teach.

Ashford Elementary School Team Leaders
(Illustrating "L" Sit)

Gymnastics is so new to our country, and there are very few private schools that teach this sport. So, almost all of the students are learning gymnastic skills for the first time. The leaders are counted on to be Coach U's right-hand helpers.

So many positive appropriations, endorsements, and turn of events begin to happen for Coach U and students in his after-school gymnastic program at Ashford Elementary School during this short period of time.

- Tumbling mats are donated for the gymnastic program to begin.

My Little Gymnast

- The after-school program is growing very fast, and the gym is filling up each day.

- The Russian Gymnastics Olympic Tour is coming to Houston in May.

- State School Demonstration at the Shamrock Hotel is scheduled for October.

- Ashford was selected as the State Demonstration School of Texas by the Texas Education Agency.

The After-School Program starts growing and overflowing with students who are filled with excitement because of Gymnastics!

Through the "grapevine," Coach U serendipitously hears a newly received, hot-off-the-press news release regarding Olga Korbut, the world-famous Olympian, Four-Gold-Metalist Russian Gymnast, and her Russian Olympic Gymnastics Team are scheduled to perform in Houston.

Coach U decides to give his elementary teaching vocation his entire repertoire of devotion (and ingenuity) and short of a miracle. He spectacularly wrangles an invitation for his after-school Gymnastics team to PRACTICE TUMBLING with the world-famous Russian Gymnastics Olympic Team!

Coach U decides to spring the news to Mar & Jac at the dinner table that very evening, "Miracles from heaven! Listen up, Mar & Jaq;

I want you both to be the first to hear the news." Mar & Jac put down their drinks and look at Coach U attentively.

Coach U excitedly exclaims, "Amazingly, after only hardly one year of creating my gymnastics program at Ashford Elementary School, we are very fortunate to be invited to warm up and tumble with none other than Olga Korbut and the Russian Gymnastics' Team in Houston!"

Coach U picks up his fork off the table and points it towards Mar & Jac, "What do you say about that, Mar & Jaq? … Because their gymnastics team is so well accepted and admired in Texas, the Russian team is coming to the United States, and one of these events will be in HOUSTON on their "Good Will Tour,"

Mar & Jac simultaneously pull back their chairs, and each bear-hug Coach U tightly around his neck, shrieking, "Awesome Dad!"

Mar & Jac are head-over-heels filled with excitement at this momentous announcement! Both ask to be excused from the table and run together out the front door to relay the thrilling news to their best friends, who live a few houses away from theirs on the same street.

The following day in Coach U's after-school class, he gathers his ever-growing, large brood of gym students, takes them aside, and proclaims in a louder-than-usual authoritative imperative, "Our after-school gymnastics team at this school has a decision to make. Ashford is chosen to participate with the Russian Gymnastics team that is touring the United States. The Russian team's first stop will be Houston just before summer.

Coach U's voice's pitch increases in intensity, "Students, do you… or do you not… want to work out in the upcoming gymnastics event?"

Mar & Jaq, along with the entire group of after-school students, answer Coach U, yelling the loudest in union with the great chorus of students in the gym, shouting at the top of their lungs, "Yes! "Yes!" Olga! Olga!"

My Little Gymnast

Coach U continues questioning his students, "Who on 'our team' is going to be selected to get to work out with Olga Korbut and the Russian Team? We have almost two months to prepare for the Russian Tour. Our Team Leaders have all the skills our team needs; their ages are 8 to 12 years old!"

As Coach U's crescendo of the emotional petition is delivered, students form a tight circle around Mar & Jaq, and Coach U. Loudly, they chant in a union, "Yes! Yes! Olga! Olga!"

Mar & Jaq practice each day with their classmates, working on form and flexibility to show the touring Russian team. All the gymnasts can now perform the "L" Sit and are so proud to show their abilities at "The Dome" (NRG Stadium).

Mar & Jaq, along with many of their friends on the team, assist Coach U in creating slogans and multiple signs showing details of the meet and drawings of "The Dome" (NRG Stadium).

The time flies by and passes so quickly as the entire school works together to prepare for the big day in the coming weeks. It seems that each day, we had television or newspaper reporters coming to our school due to the excitement of working out with the Russian Olympic Team.

We feel so special, and it is truly an honor to receive all this attention! With newspaper or television stories about our school, the more our after-school program continues to grow! Not only do we have the entire gym filled, but we are placing some mats outside since there isn't enough room in the gym.

Our numbers are really growing!

- Number of students who qualify for the Russian Tour Demo reaches twenty-two students.
- Number of "L" Sits reaches thirty students.

- Number of students who are joining the gymnastics team increases to two hundred!

"The skills you need are splits on your favorite side and three different cartwheels: A side cartwheel, a cartwheel in, and a cartwheel out. Each cartwheel needs to be completed on these lines on the gym floor. "

"I am placing numerous colorful, stripped lines on the floor so all of you students may practice your cartwheel's control on these lines."

"The cartwheels have to be performed with your hand, hand, foot, and foot, each touching the line on the floor for each of the three types of cartwheels."

Chapter 2:
Russian Tour Workout

There are so many positive experiences, awards, and accolades, but it is Olga Korbut, who is the gymnasts' SUPERSTAR of superstars, who all our students want to meet and have their photos taken with her.

Photo from the *Houston Chronicle*, March 10, 1972

(Photo taken by Houston Chronicle, March 10, 1977)
Olga Korbut (Far right) was the gymnast who seemed to ignite the sport of gymnastics in the United States. The Ashford students watched her every move!

Mar & Jaq, along with all the gymnastics students, practice rigorously for many hours each day. They are among our team members who are able to perform the necessary skills to get a chance to meet the Russian Team. Both sisters are becoming very proud of their accomplishments and push themselves, practicing daily to improve their "L" Sit skills.

The day finally comes, and all the faculty and gymnasts alike are all so excited to finally meet the Russian Team! The girls decide to wear their orange and white leotards, and the boys select their white stretch pants with suspenders over the school T-shirt.

When we arrive at NRG, there are throngs of police directing the myriads of traffic into the parking area. We are rushed onto the field area where there is a free exercise mat. An official pops up from seemingly out of nowhere and declares to us, "Gymnasts, make a line and shake hands with The Russian Gymnast Team." As our team meets the Russian Olympic Team, each Russian athlete is coupled up with one of our students and begins to warm-up by running around the mat and afterwards stretching together.

It is truly a once-in-a-lifetime experience!

dmilla Tourischcheva (on left) was the All-Around Champion for the Russian team
ıdy Vento (Student pictured on far right) was one of the Ashford students wh

Mar & Jaq are the youngest gymnasts, and they stay in the back of the staging arena, performing their gymnastics exercises together.

It was so obvious to everyone how very graceful the Russian Gymnastics Team was dancing and tumbling through their warm-ups. Each skill that they perform is a balance of power and grace! Each of our gymnasts talks excitedly about how the Russian Gymnastics Team's basic routines are being performed to perfection. Our gymnasts also notice how each of the Russian team member's physique is trim and beautiful. You can tell that they do not eat much candy, that is for sure!

The Russian Gymnastics Team is so focused while taking everything in around them. This is their first trip to the United States, and they seem to really enjoy every minute. There isn't much time spent talking and socializing between the two groups, but it is a thrill and an honor to be in the same room and sporting event with the highly decorated "World Championship Team!"

We all watch Olga's every movement, and she is smiling, it seems, the entire time she performs. Our girls are mesmerized with her throughout the entire event!

Throughout the event, the sisters are soaking everything in, and it is only when driving home they simultaneously begin spewing their excitement to Coach U and Mom, "Olga Korbut is awesome! Olga Korbut is fabulous! Olga Korbut is fantastic! Olga Korbut is the best!" and in unison shouting, "The Russian Olympic Gymnast's Team's skill level is off-the-charts!"

Mar & Jaq are jubilant with excitement, humbled to be included in this momentous event.

Chapter 3:
Joining a Gymnastic Club

After a full day at school, including participating in their after-school gymnastics workouts, at home, Mar & Jac are constantly tumbling all through the house on a daily basis, as well as retaining their excitement about the Russian Gymnastics Team. It seems that Mar & Jaq are transfixed to go everywhere doing cartwheels: going from one room too, in the driveway to the car, in the street, etc.!

Since Dad is aware of the girls' interests to learn all they can about gymnastics- and excel in the sport, and he is still their elementary school gym teacher, and he knows Coach Biron, Dad suggests that the sisters begin gymnastic lessons at Bee Gees (Biron Gymnastics) private club. Bee Gees is located between the elementary school and their house and within two miles of each other.

Both girls are not participating in any other sporting activities other than gymnastics. (They both previously started ballet and enjoyed the classes very much. They both were active as "Brownies" in the Girl Scouts and loved having to work towards goals.)

Gymnastics is going to be very challenging, as the instruction is going to be very different from anything that they have ever done before. The two main skills that Mar & Jac need to learn deal with strength and flexibility. Both girls have excellent coordination speed, and they seem to have good balance, too.

From an early start, the girls excel in different skills. Mar, who is a year and a half older than Jaq, has a great deal of strength. Jaq enjoys dancing and is very artistic in her movements. There are many gymnastic events and different equipment for each event. All the equipment is new to them since the elementary school does not have this type of equipment.

My Little Gymnast

One of the first things Mar & Jaq learn is that there are different events and specified equipment for boys and girls.

The boys have only two events, which is the same in girls' gymnastics:

Free Exercise

Rings

Parallel Bars

High Bar

Pommel Horse

Vaulting

For the girls, they had four events that needed to be learned. The events are:

Floor Exercise

Uneven Parallel Bars

Vaulting

Balance Beam

The girls toured the gym with their dad, asking many questions about each gymnastic piece of equipment. They are both so anxious and eager to get started and to learn all there is to learn about each station.

The gym is very different from their elementary gym in so many ways. The biggest difference is that it is so big!

Martin "Marty" Urand

Biron's Gymnastic Club

At their elementary school, the goal each year is to purchase ten new tumbling mats. From the pleads to the class they heard in gym class last year from Coach U and their participation in the fund-raising events that were held at the school for the purchase of new mats, Mar & Jac are aware that the mats are expensive.

Coach U tells his daughters, "Look around, girls, this gym is at least ten times larger, and the ceiling is higher than your entire school's!" The girls point out that they had never seen so many tumbling mats.

There must have been over one hundred mats all over the gym club! Some mats are in vibrant colors of the rainbow and very different in textures, shapes, and sizes. Some mats are very thick and extra soft, mostly for safety reasons.

When they come to the free exercise "floor mat," which is made of a royal blue plush carpet with a white border around the square, the girls immediately begin doing cartwheels and dancing from one corner of the gym to the other.

They are having so much fun jumping and tumbling in different directions. Mar & Jaq insist on trying out each of the pieces of equipment.

They also notice that each event does not just have one piece of equipment to practice on, but four to five pieces for each station. Especially the balance beams: They have eight high beams and eight-floor beams.

The girl's excitement grows with each step they take in the gym. When the girls and Coach U arrive at one of the gym's areas with no tumbling mats (it has a wooden floor), the girls ask, "What's this?" Coach U explains to the girls that this area is for ballet, and it is a very important part of girls' gymnastics repertoire.

Getting into the car, Mar & Jaq continue spouting their repository of questions all the way back home. As the car pulls up in the driveway, they both feel they're ready for their first class to begin.

Chapter 4:
Ashford Elementary School Focuses on A New Event

Coach U is very excited about the news he has for the gymnasts. Ashford is selected to perform at the largest Exhibit Hall in Houston. The event is scheduled for after the summer in autumn, but in this event, in order for students to participate in the demonstration, they must be able to perform an "L" Sit on the floor!

Peggy Collins performs a variation of an "L".

At present, there are only seven of Coach U's students who can hold the "L" Sit for FIVE seconds! Coach U is busy making a sign that he will place on the gym bulletin board.

The sign shows a large building; on the roof, an elementary school student is in an "L" Sit, with a large sign under the youngster. The sign states: "L you Go!" Meaning that if you can hold an "L" for five seconds, you will be part of the demonstration team that performs at the large hotel!

Each day at practice, students in each gym class practice the "L"

Sit, and slowly, students are gaining the strength to hold the difficult position. By the end of the month, there are five more students who have achieved this skill. Each time a student is successful in achieving this eminent status, their name is placed on the sign.

"We are now at 12 names with just six months remaining until the performance!" Coach U tells his large after-school group.

Mar & Jaq practice each day as well, and they are confident that they are getting closer to achieving their goals. On the way home from school each day, they happily observe many of their friends practicing in front of their homes, too.

"It's so crazy good to see all these signs in our friend's yards! Exclaims Mar to Jaq as they drive home with Coach U after school that afternoon. "Yeah, exactly Mar! I've counted 11 'L'Sit signs just in our neighborhood alone!" Jaq replies.

The girls continue to count together the number of the multitude of signs placed on the lawns in front of their neighbor's homes with the big letter "L" with their child's name on it. Seemingly, the entire neighborhood is invigorated with enthusiasm, as well as the parents of the gymnasts who accomplished the feat of holding the "L!"

By the time school begins in late August, our numbers for participation in the gymnasts' demonstration at the largest exhibit hall in Houston have certainly grown. We are now close to one hundred students!

It seems that each student who passes the test and whose name is placed on the bulletin board motivates another ten students to work even harder to earn their merit of holding the "L"!

The students get so excited for their classmates, and you can tell that it is developing a bond, a positive sportsmanship, that would make any coach proud! With each day of practice, the level of improvement is becoming contagious, and the friendships among the gymnasts are becoming an "outcome" without even trying or talking about it.

Coach U enjoys watching the students gather in the gym each morning before school to check the list to see if any of their friends passed the test. Coach U is very happily aware of this "outcome;" he feels like the less that he mentions this product, the more positive the atmosphere is at each practice.

Lately, Coach U is searching for something new, something that will create a new path for the students to take, one that still focuses on gymnastics- but doesn't create competitiveness among the students.

Then it dawns on him, why not plan and schedule a "campout" for the students? *Since I like how the gymnasts developed this high sense of teamwork and positive attitude toward each other, maybe mixing the gymnasts- and then more students can create a similar feeling? Mar & Jaq have been on several campouts and could help me at this event. As a family, we have gone to Lake Livingston for campouts for a couple of years. Now, I need to figure out how many students can safely attend an overnight campout. Sure, it would be spectacular to take the entire school, but I am sure there is a limit to how many campers would be allowed to attend.*

After receiving approval from Dr. Blackmann, the school principal, we decided to invite 100 students. That would mean two buses for fifty students and eight chaperones for each bus. We decide our criteria- the rules that fairly assess the qualifications students must pass in order to attend the event as follows: At the start of each physical education class, students will run for five minutes before class begins. At the end of each lap, students will pick up a straw. After the running period is over, students will count their total number of straws. The students with the most straws will be the top one hundred students who will be invited to the "Overnight Campout!"

The Science teacher volunteers to attend as a chaperone to lead the students on a "Nature Hike." The Librarian also volunteers to help and sign up to tell stories and give reading opportunities for the "Camp

Fire." Coach U will provide equipment for several activities during the day.

Everything is set for the Friday and Saturday night campout. Many students are motivated to participate and begin running each day in gym class to earn points for the event. Coach U is so excited that many of the runners who are excelling are not gymnasts, and the school will have a super mixture of students attending the campout and, consequently, getting opportunities to make new friendships.

Chapter 5:
Overnight Campout Big Success

By the end of March, Ashford is ready for their first campout. We rent eight cabins at Stephen F. Austin State Park in Sealy, Texas. The students bring their sleeping bags and lunch kits filled with their favorite snacks to get them through the evening!

We have sixty boys and forty girls earn the straws they need to qualify for this major school event. The students sign up for the events that they want to participate in on Saturday morning and afternoon. Nature hiking is one of the favorites, along with arts and crafts classes. There are lots of kickball and parachute games, and of course, a wonderful campfire for cooking marshmallows and a scary story or two by the school librarian.

The bottom line is that Ashford can offer a social event where students have an opportunity to enjoy recreation with their peers. (I later heard many stories throughout the year from students who went camping for the first time with their families because of the new outdoor experiences that so many students got to experience at the Campout!)

Jaq shows her handstand during swim break.

Chapter 6:
Shamrock Demonstration

The day finally comes, and all of Ashford's gymnasts line up in front of the school to load the six buses to head downtown. The final count is 324 gymnasts who are able to perform the sitting "L" position!

It is almost unbelievable that so many elementary school students worked so hard to accomplish this difficult task. It just shows that when you work hard and believe in yourself, you can do almost anything! Coach U is so very proud of each gymnast and proud of his students' determination and dedication to the gymnastics team each has shown over the last several months.

The gymnasts enter the Ballroom from six different doors. They march into the Ballroom to the music of the Olympic theme. Each of the 324 students is also so proud and strong, with a smile on each of their faces.

The team takes their assigned places on the beautiful, luxurious carpets and is spaced out across the entire Ballroom. The spectators are teachers and administrators from all over Texas, parents, friends, and neighbors, and a few reporters and photographers. The guests are sitting in chairs around the outside of the carpet areas. There must be twenty-five hundred spectators! They are so excited to see this many young, poised elementary school students all dressed in leotards and, shorts and T-shirts for the boys. The team of youngsters is all so mature, as they wait for the music to begin and the que to start their routine. The music is "Jesus Christ Super Star," and when it begins, all the students kick up to a handstand. After a beat or so, the team does a forward roll into a straddle. Some of the team tumble into a front split and then begin in sync with each beat of the music.

And then stretching. All at once, it happens! What we were all waiting for and practiced so hard for: We waited for that certain beat, and three hundred and twenty- four students lifted themselves up into the "L" position off the floor!! The crowd seemed to have clapped for eons.

By the time the students hit the finale of our "Live and Let Die" routine (soundtrack to the 8th James Bond film of the same name- written by Paul and Linda McCartney and performed by Paul McCartney and Wings), the audience of relatives, neighbors, children of friends, etc., is on their feet- standing in awe of their daughters, and sons, who performs the routines perfectly!

Coach U, now teary-eyed, turns and whispers to the videographer, "Because of the elation I'm feeling; I'm absolutely thrilled with my students' performances; I can't see if others are crying, but I am told that there isn't a dry eye in attendance!" The videographer whispers back, "Yes, that's right, Coach U, there's not a dry eye in the audience!"

Mar & Jac, along with the other 322 team members, receive adoration, admiration, and impromptu autograph sessions. The gymnasts sign their autographs all the way to the buses!

Before Coach U gets on one of the buses, he accepts an interview from a news reporter attending the Shamrock Ballroom event. Coach U shakes the interviewer's hand and answers the reporter's question, "How did he and his newly trained elementary school gymnastics students pull this off?"

Coach U clears his voice and replies, "I expect a lot of discipline from the students, but the children always give even more of themselves to gymnastics than I ask. Now that the team has grown by leaps and bounds, my expectations for the gymnastics team have grown even more. I know that I personally have grown from this experience too, but it is the students themselves who have learned an even better lesson- by seeing the success from all their hard work."

It has been said, but I am not sure by whom, "To never

underestimate the heart of a champion." Coach U added, "And never set expectations for your students." If students are motivated, there is no telling what they can achieve! Coach U has always had a negative feeling toward those who do not have high expectations for others, especially children.

Chapter 7:
Extraordinary Tumbling Routine "Live and Let Die"

By the end of the school year, our tumbling team is really improving! We have created a tumbling/beam routine that we demonstrated at the Shamrock Hotel. Coach U planned for the gymnastics team to perform this routine at another event in the most popular mall in Houston, and it received standing ovations from the audience! Today, Coach U has another amazing event up his sleeve!

This event, like practicing and tumbling with the Russian Gymnastic Team, is truly spectacular, too! Coach U says our reputation has grown, and our team has received numerous invitations to perform in this upcoming event. Our next event is a two-year contract with the Houston Rockets to perform at Half-time of their games! Coach U really outdid himself with our next performance, and it is going to be pretty spectacular!

The mats are placed in an "X," and the routine begins with twenty girls in a circle around the "X." With each beat of the music, the gymnasts move from the circle to four lines, one at each corner of the "X." There is one boy, Greg Peters, who enters the tumbling lines. He is a dynamic tumbler who has a huge "back-tuck" that is really "Sky-high." With just a few beats to the music, Greg does his magical tumbling over four girls and lands in the middle of the "X." It was just ssssspectacular!

My Little Gymnast

Ashford Elementary was a favorite at the Houston Rockets NBA games performing at half time each season.

Chapter 8:
First Day of Gymnastic School

Heading to Biron's Gymnastic from Katy is just a short drive away. It is the first day of Gymnastics school for the girls. The gym looks very different, as the entire gym is filled with boys and girls- either getting ready for their classes or teams that are practicing.

Mar & Jaq are sitting in the gym's waiting area watching all the activities and other gymnasts. They are so used to seeing their dad as the only coach in the school that it is interesting to them that there are numerous coaches in the gym. Also, there are so many different pieces of gymnastics equipment, and at each station is a coach. The girls count 20 coaches in the gym!

It is 4 o'clock, and their class started. Mar & Jaq begin with running around the free exercise mat and then do exercises such as push-ups sit-ups, and working on their splits and other exercises that will improve their flexibility.

Mar starts off on the uneven bars. They are learning pullovers. Jaq goes to the floor balance beam and begins learning how to walk with the correct posture from one end to the other. Jaq's arms are over her head in a circular movement while one leg is dipping low, and her other leg pointing her toes to take the next step.

This is their first event, other than tumbling, that they are participating in their lives. Coach U looks over at the girls and can see from the expressions on their faces how pleased they are- taking their turns and listening to their coaches give them instructions. Coach U says to himself, As I watch them, I am learning as well since all I really knew about gymnastics was tumbling,

The whistle blows, and the girls march to their next station. Mar to beam and Jaq to the floor. Mar does the same movements as her sister while Jaq is learning forward-and-backward rolls on a mat shaped like a wedge that they call the "Cheese Mat." It is similar to a triangle with the flat side down and the top going down- so that it helps the students roll down the wedge. All the student gymnasts really enjoy tumbling on the "Cheese!"

For their final rotation, Mar goes to the floor, and Jaq starts her first time vaulting. They are working on a "tuck vault." The students' first practice is running down the vault path and jumping on a springboard with two feet. Their coach tells the students to believe they are jumping into a water puddle when they land on the springboard. After a few practice runs and springboard take-offs, the gymnasts begin learning how to do a tuck-vault over the "Horse."

The "Tuck" is next after leaving the springboard, and students place both hands on the horse and bring their knees to their chest while going over the horse and landing on two feet on large soft mats.

At the conclusion of the last event, the student gymnasts go back on the floor exercise mat and begin their flexibility stretching. They stretch for ten minutes, working on splits on each side, as well as arm and shoulder stretches.

The class is ninety minutes and meets on Monday, Wednesday, and Friday.

Within six months, Mar & Jaq are promoted to a developmental team that is made of girls that are ages six and under. They are given pink, long-sleeved leotards, and the name of the team is "Pinkies." There are fifteen girls selected, and their classes will be two hours long, three days per week! The girls are elated to have made the team and to receive more gymnastic instruction each week!

When Mar & Jaq hear that their new coach will be their dad, they are joyous at the good news. The owner, Beau Biron, and Coach U became good friends and even talked about opening a Gymnastic Club in Katy, the town west of Houston, where the Urands have just moved.

Within the next 6 months, the girls are progressing so well with the Pink Team, and Ashford Elementary is getting ready for the BeeGee Extravaganza.

They have practiced every day at school for the three different performances they are going to perform, as well as three workouts at Bee Gees (Biron Gymnastics).

With each day, the school becomes more and more excited about the exhibition that is going to take place in one week. The girls are very tired when they come home each day. They get a quick dinner, do their homework, and go right to sleep.

When the weekend comes around, Mar & Jaq will catch up on their school studies, read a lot, and, of course, rest!

Chapter 9:
A New Elementary School

The girls not only have a new gymnastic school to prepare for, but they are moving to Katy, Texas, ten miles away. It is their first move in their life, and they are experiencing so many different positive and negative emotions that it feels like they are riding an emotional roller coaster. One of the positive emotions they are feeling is that they are both looking forward to meeting so many new friends.

Mar & Jaq, and Coach U finish out the year, saying goodbye to students and teachers as they move to a new neighborhood and school. Coach U trains another coach who has gymnastic experience and a very similar background to himself. His name is Ashley Glass, and he picks up where Coach U finished!

The new school is West Memorial Elementary School. It is in an area that is under a lot of new residential construction. Our house is a new house that we have been waiting to be finished. It is one of ten homes on our street that is under construction to be built, and we're so excited to move into the very first house that we will own, not rent.

Coach U is also moving to a new school as well. Everyone in the family is so excited and happy about the possibilities of all the new experiences that we have ahead of us.

The school is for Kindergarten to Fifth-grade students. Mar is going into the fourth grade, and Jaq is going into the second grade.

Chapter 10:
Mar & Jaq Change Gymnastic Clubs

By the end of the school year, there are big plans made by Beau Biron and Coach U. They decide to start a gymnastics club in Katy, within a mile of West Memorial Elementary School.

Coach Biron donates some of his older equipment and finances the start-up of Katy Kips Gymnastic Club. The space that they find is a storefront with a long glass window in the front. It was a few stores down from Gerlands' Food Fair and is very conveniently located, with plenty of parking.

The area is 4,000 square feet with a bathroom. It is a very small area, as far as gymnasiums go! However, each event is scaled down to fit the small area. Coach U feels like it is a "Start-Up Gym" for an area that does not have a gymnastics club.

There is one set of uneven bars in the back portion of the gym. A smaller runway for vaulting is on the side of the gym. The balance beam is in front of the windows, and the "smaller" floor version is for the "Free" exercise routines.

Beau Biron and Coach U Start a New Business Called Katy Kips Gymnastic Club

Chapter 11:
A New Gymnastic Club for Katy, Texas

The Katy Gymnastic Club on Mason Road in Katy

The Gym is the only one in Katy, and the little storefront is filled with young gymnasts. Mar & Jaq are now in the fourth and second grades and working out more than ever! All their friends from their school in Katy are also taking gymnastics classes with them, and before long, we start our first team!

The gymnastics team chooses to name the team "Kips!" A Kip is the name of a movement that is accomplished on either the girl's uneven bars or the boy's high bar. It is a swinging motion under the bar that requires a lot of strength to propel one to a "support" position on the bar. It seems that it is a challenging movement that few gymnasts can perform, and the new Katy gymnastics team chooses that name for their team's name. Henceforward, we are known as the Katy "Kips."

Mar & Jaq's First Team at Katy "Kips" Gymnastics Club

The First Katy Team and They Named Themselves the "Kips."

The Kips practice each day from 6:00-9:00 pm. These young athletics work and train very hard!

My Little Gymnast

*The "Kips" First Coaching Staff: (LtoR)
Jodie, Steve, John, and Coach U*

With all the practice and learning new routines, the team is ready to compete against other clubs. This tiny gym is being transformed into a competitive gym for the four main events for girls/women's gymnastics.

Chapter 12:
West Memorial Elementary School Receives an Outstanding Award

With the new gym going well and growing, the Physical Education program is reaching new goals as well. The school has a great principal who loves sports and physical activity. She wants a well-rounded school.

Demonstration School Selected by the Texas Education Agency

(L to R) Student Council Scott Draper, Superintendent Brown, Trustee Alexander, Principal Thompson, Physical Education Teachers Pat Unruh, Natalie Rankin, Coach U, and Student President Maggie Smith

Series 2:
Mar & Jaq Compete in their First Meet

Mar begins to gain the judge's approval in excelling in Vaulting and uneven bars. During a meet, Mar's strength carries her through an uneven bar and she becomes known in the city for breaking a wooden rail during her routine.

Jaq loves to dance and begins to place in Gold on Beam and the Floor. Competition never really heats up between the sisters. (Makes Dad Happy)

www.ingramcontent.com/pod-product-compliance
Lightning Source LLC
Chambersburg PA
CBHW041322110526
44591CB00021B/2872